Mrs.
Miller

The
Country Mail
Is Coming

The Country Mail Is Coming

 POEMS FROM  DOWN UNDER

by Max Fatchen
with illustrations by Catharine O'Neill

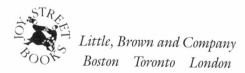

Little, Brown and Company
Boston   Toronto   London

First U.S. Edition

First published in 1987 in Australia by Omnibus Books

Library of Congress Cataloging-in-Publication Data

Fatchen, Max. The country mail is coming: poems from
down under / by Max Fatchen: with illustrations by
Catharine O'Neill. p. cm. Summary: In this collection
of poems, the author relates his experiences growing up
in the Australian countryside. ISBN 0-316-27493-3
1. Country life — Juvenile poetry. 2. Children's poetry,
Australian. [1. Country life — Poetry. 2. Australian
poetry.] I. O'Neill, Catharine, ill. II. Title.
PR9619.3.F38C68 1990 821 — dc20 89-31654
CIP AC

Joy Street Books are published by Little, Brown
and Company (Inc.)

BP

10 9 8 7 6 5 4 3 2 1

Published simultaneously in Canada
by Little, Brown & Company (Canada) Limited

Printed in the United States of America

For my grandchildren Jessica,
Nicholas, Dominic, Jonathan, Claire
and Sarah and for my friends next-
door, Annmarie, Tommy, André,
Raymond, Matthew, Janine and
Anne-Marie and also for Pauline Fietz,
not forgetting Magoo,
the dog, and Rufus the cat.

DAVID LAMPLOUGH

Max Fatchen and friends —
granddaughter Jessica and friend Annmarie

CONTENTS

SUMMER MAIL

The country mail is coming
Across the wilting land,
Through summer's dancing hazes
And slyly shifting sand.

The country mailman's whistling,
With elbow out the side,
His dog upon the mailbag
With watchful canine pride.

And while the mail truck's jolting
Where stony creek bed shelves,
You'll hear the mailbag's letters
All talk among themselves . . .

. . . "We've added to the kitchen
And thanks for sending cups . . .
"Belinda's had her baby . . .
The heeler's had her pups . . .

. . . "The shearing shed's got termites . . .
We wondered if you'd heard . . ."

The letters go on talking
With word on whispered word . . .

"It's lonely in the city . . .
For home a bloke gets sick . . .
"I hear the bull took after Mum . . .
I'm glad that she was quick . . .

"I miss the country mornings . . .
I miss my old straw hat . . ."
The mailman keeps on driving
While still the letters chat.

. . . "Dear Sir, on payment of account
We felt we should enquire,
A box of nails, two milking pails . . .
A roll of fencing wire . . ."

. . . "Dear Gran, will you remember,
That I'll be eight next week . . ."
The mailman's truck is grinding
Across another creek.

While letter after letter
Recites its humble tale,
That's if you dare to listen
To bags that carry mail.

The mailman's reached the township
His old truck starts to slow.
A world is in his mailbag.
I wonder, does he know?

AT SUNRISE

Across the silent paddock
There comes a cautious hare,
His ears, two pointed fingers,
To probe the frosty air.
And where the wheat is growing
He pauses in his run
Along the aisles of morning,
To breakfast with the sun.

PRECIOUS

On webs the evening spiders spun
The drops of dew now catch the sun,
In shining strands they glisten there,
Those morning pearls my fences wear.

IN A WHIRL

Willy-nilly, round and round,
Whirlwind swirling from the ground,
Picking up its bits of paper,
In a skywards-spinning caper.
With a whistle and a howl,
Waltzing with a squawking fowl,
Snatching clothes from whizzing line.
Some of them, I fear, are mine.

Slamming doors and rattling tin
Goes this windy larrikin.
Joyous in the air it flings
Multitudes of dizzy things,
Shoals of leaves from blowing boughs,
Hats it snatched from children's brows,
Wrapped around with dusty banners,
Whirlwinds have such awful manners.

Thieving, swirling tower of dirt,
You went and stole my Sunday shirt.

CRUNCHY

With all that morning fiber
And breakfast bran to greet me
I keep away from horses
In case they want to eat me!

DO IT YOURSELF

"**O**h, please will you hold baby,
It's such a little dear."
But let them keep on asking,
For, frankly I stand clear . . .
That burping and that crowing
Well, this is how I view it,
It's bad enough just knowing
That I'm related to it.

15

WINDY WORK

Weary breeze through my window screen,
Where are you going and where have you been?

. . . I cooled the sweat on a farmer's brow
And fanned the dreams of a dozing cow.
I played a tune in the telephone wires
And rocked the trees for the magpie choirs.
I shook the stalks of the long-eared wheat
And they danced the paddock off its feet.

I passed a train with its diesel smell.
I caught the clang of the crossing bell.
I tumbled the bushes and made them roll
And fluttered the flag on a school-yard pole.
I carried the children's lunch-hour shout
No wonder a breeze is a bit puffed out.

I rushed and rippled a placid dam.
I stroked the grass and here I am.
I climbed the range and each rock-ridged hill.
So may I rest on your windowsill?

GATE GOSSIP

I like our gate,
Its sturdy charm
That guards the entrance
To our farm.

It's nice when shut,
Or open wide,
To sit upon
Or sit astride.

But gates are there
With things to do

19

Like letting sheep
And cattle through.

Our gate has bars
With several bends
From careless cars
Of farming friends.

The gateposts lean,
A little tired,
With fences stretching
Rusty-wired.

A country gate
Is surely best
To prop a farmer
For his rest.

With one foot up,
And elbows flat
Now who could pass
A man like that?

While every bit
Of iron will ring,
With all the
Rural gossiping.

The magpies fly
To sunset tree.
A voice impatient
Calls to tea.

Then, whistling,
Home the farmer goes
As gate
And conversation
Close.

THE MILKER

Up and down,
Squeeze and squirt,
Milky splashes
On my shirt.
Tug and press,
Down and up,
Creamy streams
For can and cup.
Custards, puddings,
Ice cream, cheese,
Brim the bucket
At my knees.
Milky marvel,
Tasty tides.
Praise the cow
And her insides.

Down and up,
Squirt and squeeze.
(Mine's a chocolate malted,
Please.)

THUD

The roller skates that Mary had
Were borrowed by her foolish dad.
He'll never make a brilliant skater,
Or so the doctor told us later.

CALLING ALL CARS

All areas were notified.
It seemed a puzzling case.
The raspberry ripple ice cream tub
Had vanished without trace.

A tub of most exquisite brand
And only newly bought.
Identikits were quickly scanned
And witnesses were sought.

The motive? It was surely greed
And those who probe and pry
Can be a shrewd and dogged breed
Who test each alibi.

For suddenly the breakthrough came
But only just in time.
Within an ear, a whispered name
Connected with the crime.

And so we happily report
That, by informers branded,
The criminal has now been caught
Red-raspberry-ripple-handed.

SILLY BILLY

When Billy blew his bubble gum
It grew like some enormous moon.
It lifted him with frightening speed,
A sticky and a green balloon.

So upwards, upwards Billy soared
Until he reached tremendous heights.
It broke all records they could find
For unrestricted bubble flights.

But I am very much afraid
The bubble burst, the gum was popped,
And now they work with scoop and spade
To fill the hole where Billy dropped.

Indeed, I think the time has come
When you should act on this assumption,
That people, blowing bubble gum,
Should use a little bubble gumption.

SHAKES AND LADDERS

As a leaning
ladder
climber
there are careful
steps to take.
Surely nothing
can be sadder
if a careless
move you make.
Do not slither,
Do not stumble
or your nerves
can come unstrung
and you well
may take
a tumble
if you miss
another rung.
If you're lost
upon a ladder
do not think
this statement
rude.
If you only
took
your bearings
you might learn
your
laddertude.

DOWN AND UP

Words	top.
are	very
nice	the
to	reach
speak	you
and	until
read	stop
and	never
some	and
are	along
very	read
long	so
indeed	play
and	to
if	out
you	come
are	us
the	like
reading	words
age	for
you'll	way
reach	different
the	a
bottom	quite
of	going
this	we're

page. Now read across. We'd like to say

ANYONE WANTING A FIERY DRAGON?

With a sulphur smell,
The air grew hot
As the dragon steamed
On the used-car lot.

"Genuine scales,
A spiky tail,"
The notice said,
"This beast for sale.

"Belches flame
In a crimson sheet,

And guarantees
A steady heat.

"Huge and fearless,
Brave and bold,
And thermostatically
Controlled.

"It's careful not
To sear or scorch.
Use as a heater
Or a torch.

"Warmer than
A blacksmith's forge,
And recommended
By Saint George."

I bought the beast,
What else to do?
Now you should see
My barbecue!

IS THIS YOURS?

The gecko sometimes sheds its tail
In danger or distress.
How careless of it not to leave
A forwarding address!

DINOSAUR DEPARTMENT

Clever Clem went out of doors,
Playing with the dinosaurs,
Telling others in his class,
"Not to worry. They eat grass."
A snap, a CRUNCH! The sad news breaks
That clever boys can make mistakes.

BRAIN DRAIN

The dinosaurs did not remain
Because they had a tiny brain.
But recently, our teacher found
That tiny brains are still around . . .

WHO'S THERE?

If you hear a dinosaur
Knocking loudly on your door,
Through the keyhole firmly say
"Nobody is home today."
If the bell should start to ring,
Tell the beast, "No visiting."
If you see there's more than one,
Turn around and start to run.

STRICTLY FOR THE BIRDS

Our water hole should suit quite well
The birds that seek a swish-sh-sh motel.
It's ideal as a stopping place
For herons with their stilt-like grace,
The surface smooth to land upon
For passing duck or weary swan.

A fine cuisine, secluded trees,
And yes, we have some vacancies.
No fancy frills, but nice and quiet.
Are frogs and crickets on your diet?
Or, if another dish you need,
We serve a juicy waterweed.

We like to set a decent tone
For feather bedding, bring your own.
A four-star rating? Let us say
Our stars include the Milky Way
And while accommodation's damp
The moon can be your reading lamp.

Our hospitality's well-meaning.
Facilities include dry preening
And, if you're only overnight,
We'll see you catch your early flight.

YOU RANG?

My father thinks the telephone
Is something better left alone.
His attitude? Do please excuse it.
He never gets a chance to use it.

WHOA

Eleanor rides a piebald horse
That's very wise and knowing
And when it pulls up short . . . of course
Eleanor keeps on going.

TIDE TALK

The tide and I had stopped to chat
About the waves where seabirds sat,
About the yachts with bobbing sails
And quite enormous, spouting whales.

The tide has lots to talk about.
Sometimes it's in. Sometimes it's out.
For something you must understand,
It's up and down across the sand;
Sometimes it's low and sometimes high.
It's very wet and never dry.

The tide, quite crossly, said: "The sea
Is always out there pushing me.
And just when I am feeling slack,
It sends me in then drags me back.
It never seems to let me go.
I rise. I fall. I'm to and fro."

I told the tide, "I know it's true
For I am pushed around like you.
And really do they think it's fair?
Do this. Do that. Come here. Go there."

Then loudly came my parents' shout.
So I went in.
                    The tide went out.

BUT WHY NOT?

She comes at four to rap the door
And asking who will play?
Please, Annmarie. It cannot be,
No visiting today.

For Lucy, with her homework,
Is making awful scenes,
While Martha's lumps could well be mumps
And Albert's split his jeans.

With Arthur's bathroom drawings
I'm not exactly smitten,
While mother cat, on our best mat
Has had another kitten.

The fridge has just defrosted.
The spuds are boiling dry.
That fearful, smoking ruin
Was once an apple pie.

The telephone keeps ringing,
The gurgling sink is blocked.
The car keys are . . . inside the car
Which now, alas, I've locked.

The kitchen is a bedlam,
So all that I can say,
No, Annmarie . . . WOE, Annmarie,
No visiting today.

UNCLE FRED

Uncle Fred with glares and stitches
Constantly repairs his britches.
Though he tries a larger fitting
Uncle Fred is always splitting,
Every straining seam expanding,
All his efforts notwithstanding.

Oh, the ripping and the rending.
More repairs, alas, are pending.
Fat men who insist on bending
Can't expect a happy ending.

BE WARNED

I always get into a stew
With people who read in the loo.
No wonder I rage
As they're turning each page
For the rest of us want to go, too.

SEA THING

It may be stretching things a bit
But on this page an eel won't fit,
And that's because, it should be stated,
An eel is so darned eeeeeeeeeeeeeeeeeeeeeeeeeeeeeelongated.

AND S-S-SO TO B-B-BED

"**D**o go to bed," they're saying,
But do they know what's there,
Within that crowded darkness
Or shrieking through the air?

What's that upon the bedrail?
What's hiding underneath?
There could be miles of crocodiles
With big, expectant teeth.

"Now go to bed this instant!"
But have they ever dared
The shadows in the passageway?
Were parents *never* scared?

"Now into bed." Their voices
Are rising to a shout.
But when they turn the light off
It's then the THINGS come out!

ARE YOU IN THERE?

It's what I've been dreading
And who would rejoice
On hearing those footsteps
The tone in that voice?
And what to reply,
For it's laden with doom —
That terrible cry
"Have you tidied your room?"

HERE, PUSS

We have
a sitting-
straight
cat,
a trim
and tabby
friend.   end.
Our cat   one
won't fuss.   at
She purrs at us and curls up

HELP!

Any magazines
With scenes
Or information
On transportation,
population,
inflation,
marine parks,
or sharks?
Any clues
or news
on political views
Or Who's Who's?

Anything about
statistics,
national characteristics,
mountain ranges,
climatic changes,
hiking,
or the Viking?

Any slides
on tides,
wading birds,
herds,
or Kurds?

What about
The race
in space,
flora,
or an aurora?

Any files
on crocodiles?

If you haven't looked
For goodness' sake, DO!

On Friday morning
My project's due.

OUCH

Meredith likes hockey.
She nearly always wins.
She's fast. She's tall.
She whacks the ball
And everybody's shins.

JUST FRIENDS

A cockroach hasn't many friends
And neither has the rhino.
I know which one I'd sooner have
To live beneath our lino.

AT THE BEACH

Our holiday activities
Have frantic, swimming strokes
With ice-creamed lips and sailing ships
And endless kiosk Cokes.
With sanded towels and gritty rugs
Among the seaside throngs
Where eager dogs mouth tennis balls
And people lose their thongs.
The mix-up with our salad lunch
We hardly like to raise,
The lettuce smeared with sunburn cream
Our backs with mayonnaise!

IRON MAN

Proud on his board,
Surf-wise and brave
There goes my father
Riding a wave.
A flurry of legs,
The sea in a lather,
And there goes the wave,
Riding my father.

I SAY!

Cockatoos are talkative
And readily converse.
But words they speak
Through cheeky beak
Can go from bird to worse.

BIG MOUTH

The clam, it seems, is well equipped
For staying very tightly lipped
Although, about a year ago
One tried a rather curt "Hullo."
So now they've banned it from the rocks
For being such a chatterbox.

PLAYING DIRTY

The Romans built their road and path
And also built the Roman bath.
Their enemies had little hope,
For what is worse than swords?
              Why, soap.

WISH YOU WERE HERE

We're sending you this saucy card
We hope you find it funny.
We'll also send you heaps of love
If you send heaps of money.

Our guest house has this one delight,
Banana custard every night.
No wonder, after such a meal,
I suddenly begin to peel.

Here's Albert in his bathers,
There isn't any doubt,
While some of him is in them,
That most of him is out.

Eric liked to spend the day
Eating at the takeaway.
But this was Eric's big mistake.
The chairs his weight began to break
Until, with pulleys and a derrick,
They had to takeaway poor Eric.

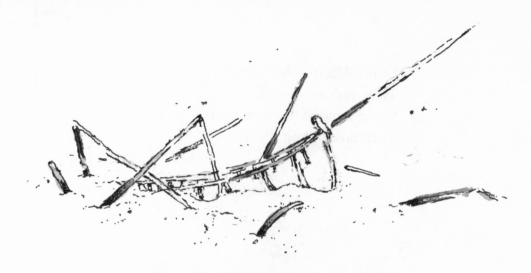

CHILDREN LOST

On a lonely beach the old wreck lies
With its rusted ribs and sides,
To the biting lash of the salty wind
And the drive of the flooding tides.

Years ago it was wrecked, they said,
Wrecked where the loud winds blew.
All hands were lost in the sad affair
And the women and children too.

It's there I went on a moonlit night
Where the cliffs slope wild and steep,
And suddenly came a shout and cry
As the ship awoke from sleep.

She had her masts and sails again,
No longer a broken wreck
While the sailors sang as they hauled the ropes
And the children played on the deck.

They shouted and played on the heaving deck
Or sat at their cabin tea
While the sly winds filled the swelling sails
On the toss of the cunning sea.

But no one knew and no one dreamed . . .
Beware of the sailor's boast
That says he's master of the sea
Or king of the rugged coast.

For I heard it all on a moonlit night,
The eager waves' wild roar
And the cries of the crew as the great sea threw
That broken ship ashore.

Where, where the children? Never a sound
On the reef's cold rock and stone
For the selfish sea had taken them all
And kept them for its own.

"Perhaps, perhaps . . ." the sea kings said
To the children deep and drowned,
"We will let you go to the shore again
But by this bond you're bound.

"That you are the children of the sea,
Of the waves and the dolphin's track
On a moonlit night we'll set you free
But then we'll call you back . . .

"On the ghostly beach you will play your games
But far from the cheerful town
Then back we'll call you, children, back
When the cold-eyed moon goes down."

Or so it seemed to come to me
In the voice of the wind and the tide
As I stood on the beach where the moonlight fell
On the ship with the broken side.

And did I hear and could I hear
The sound of some voices there?
Did figures form and vanish again
In the strange and haunted air?

How shall I tell you what I felt
And how will you understand
What, by the moon, my own eyes saw —
Small footprints in the sand!

SILHOUETTES

I saw a swan in the evening glide
And then another by its side
Then came a line, a feathered fleet
That sailed where moon and water meet
As, one by one and bird by bird,
The glinting waves they gently stirred.
Across the lake their course they set,
Necks curving in a silhouette
Until I could not hear at all,
The drifting music of their call.
But when it came my time to sleep
I counted swans instead of sheep.